# Boston Beanpot Cookery

*Copyright© 1996 by Vincent F. Zarrilli*

Printed in the United States of America
Library of Congress Catalog _____ No. 96-25159
ISBN 1-891827-00-6

### Published By:
The Pot Shop
Box 101, Hanover Station
Boston, MA 02113
(617) 523-9210
Fax (617) 523-6765
www.potshopofboston.com

### Cover Illustration By:
Wendy J. Baker

**BAKER DESIGN**
CUSTOM ILLUSTRATION
www.bakerdesign.us

D0920466

# TABLE OF CONTENTS

# TABLE OF CONTENTS

# TABLE OF CONTENTS

# Introduction

Throughout its history, Boston has been linked to beans. Surely the lowly legume is not the sort of association city forefathers would have sought when striving to cast their city's mark in the New World.

But find each other they did — as evidenced by the names Beantown, Boston baked beans, Beanpot Hockey Tourney and the Boston bean pot, among others.

It hasn't been until the 1990s, however, with its emphasis on healthful eating, that the homey image of a bubbling pot of beans has gained cache. Beans are of the moment, the very definition of what our food should be about — carbohydrate and fiber rich. The fondue pots and huge electric skillets of earlier eras have been replaced by the traditional stoneware bean pot, the most potent image your kitchen can display to show that you are eating "right" for our times.

The bean of Boston is, of course, the Boston Baked Bean, a mélange of small (usually navy or pea) beans spiked with salt pork, mustard and maple syrup or molasses. The origin of the dish comes from the Puritan prohibition against working on the Sabbath, a period they set from sundown Saturday to sundown Sunday.

Although much prose and poetry testifying to the "divine" nature of (good) food suggests otherwise, to the early Massachusetts Bay colonizers, cooking was base human labor and thus not allowed during periods of prolonged worship.

On the other hand, even Puritan appetites could be urgent. How to best satisfy hunger without defying sanctity? A blast of heavenly trumpets, please, to herald — ta, ta — the baked bean.

*i*

The one-pot meal, consisting mainly of peas or beans, was already a staple in the English diet before their arrival in America. The Native Americans also cooked indigenous beans in a "pot" made in a special hole in the ground. The colonists maintained this simple tradition, adding cured pork (bacon) and a little of the native sugar (maple) to the pot for enrichment and flavor, its long, slow cooking (baked beans are almost impossible to overcook) adapted beautifully to the colonists' need to start the cooking Saturday afternoon and then just leave the pot over the slowly dying fire until they consumed it, hopefully still warm, later that day or at Sunday morning breakfast before the hours spent at church.

Fanny Farmer, in the earliest editions of her famous cookbook, tells us that the reason the baked beans and Boston formed such a firmly wedded pair is due to the local development of the traditional bean baking pot which so perfectly suited the beans cooking requirements.

She writes, "The fine reputation which Boston Baked Beans have gained has been attributed to the earthen bean-pot with small top and bulging sides in which they are supposed to be cooked." As a bonus, she added, the pot's ability to retain heat helps keep the beans warm after they are cooked and the fire has gone out, thus helping to keep the Sabbath holy.

Baked beans kept their popularity in the colonies long after the Puritans were dispersed. Old-fashioned Yankee thrift is as good a rationale as any for their continued appeal. Thrift and the fact that beans advance preparation meant that the cook could enjoy the meal around which they were consumed as well as anyone else.

Puritans often shared a communal oven for the preparation of their Saturday bean meals, thereby conserving on scarce fuel while offering a rare chance to socialize. The Saturday night church bean supper gave way to beans on Saturdays in a majority of private homes. Slab bacon was replaced by a chunk of salt pork in the cooking and hot dogs in the eating of the beans. Through the early part of this century, a Saturday bean wagon would circulate through Boston and its environs selling already hot, cooked beans from one box and brown bread and sweets from another, so thoroughly distributing this preferred food that Boston acquired its most famous nickname, Beantown.

From its New England roots, baked beans and others of the region's foods, spread west with the migration pattern, which populated the nation. In fact, according to the classic Time-Life book of American Cooking, "New England cooking may exist today in purer form in parts of the Dakotas, the Northwest or even Alaska than it does in those areas of the East vacated long ago by the original Yankees and inhabited now by people of Polish, Italian, Irish, or Portuguese descent."

As you look through the recipes in this book, influences from those cultured as well as traditional staples will be found. All have been adapted to modern palates and will be best if prepared in the brown glazed, 2½ quart, Official Boston Bean Pot. This classically designed pot easily holds recipes using one pound of dried beans. Bean-free casseroles and vegetable dishes designed for preparation in the official pot have also been included.

## Bean preparation tips:

—    A one-pound package of dry beans yields five to six cups of cooked beans.

—    Pick over the dried beans for any small stones, sticks or other foreign matter. Rinse well in a colander.

—    Soaking is necessary before use. Either cover the rinsed beans with 2 quarts of water and soak 10 to 12 hours. Or, cover beans by two inches with water. Bring to boil and cook for 2 to 3 minutes. Cover and leave off heat for 2 hours. In either case, drain beans from soaking water before cooking to improve digestibility (although some nutrients will be lost). Add fresh water to cook. Most beans will cook in one to three hours, or follow directions with specific recipe.

—    The Official Boston Bean Pot can be used in a moderate oven or on top of the stove, but only with a heat diffuser at a low temperature.

**— Merilyn DeVos**

# Boston Baked Beans

| | |
|---|---|
| 1lb. | (2 cups) Dry navy beans |
| 1½ | Quarts cold water |
| 1 | Teaspoon salt |
| 1/3 | Cup brown sugar |
| 1 | Teaspoon dry mustard |
| ¼ | Cup molasses |
| ¼lb. | Salt pork |
| 1 | Medium onion, sliced |

1. Rinse beans; add to cold water.
2. Bring to boil; simmer 2 minutes; remove from heat; cover, let stand 1 hour. (Or, add beans to water; let soak overnight).
3. Add salt to beans and soaking water; cover; simmer until tender, about 1 hour.
4. Drain, reserving liquid.
5. Measure 1¾ cups bean liquid, adding water if needed. Combine with next four ingredients.
6. Cut salt pork in half; score one half, set aside. Grind or thin-slice remainder.
7. In beanpot, alternate layers of beans, onion, ground salt pork, and sugar mixture. Repeat. Top with scored salt pork.
8. Cover; bake at 300° for 5-7 hours. Add more liquid if needed.

Makes 8 servings.

* Baked kidney beans, substituting kidney beans for navy or pea beans.

# Zucchini Casserole

2      Large firm zucchini
2      Beaten eggs
¼      Cup bread crumbs
1      Small grated onion
4      Tablespoons butter, melted
¼      Cup grated Parmesan cheese
      Salt and pepper to taste

1. Cut off tips of zucchini, slice in ¼ inch rounds. Cook in small amount of salted water until soft. Drain and mash coarsely.

2. In a bowl, combine the eggs, bread crumbs, onion, salt and pepper. Mix well. Stir in the melted butter to coat the bread crumbs. Add zucchini and stir gently.

3. Pour mixture into bean-pot. Sprinkle with cheese. Bake at 350° for 30 minutes.

Serves 6

# Beef Goulash

| | |
|---|---|
| 2lbs. | Beef stew meat, cut in 1½ inch chunks |
| ½ | Cup butter |
| 2 | Teaspoons ground marjoram |
| 1 | Teaspoon caraway seeds |
| 1 | Teaspoon lemon peel |
| 6 | Large onions, sliced |
| 1 | 6 oz. can tomato paste |
| 1 | Tablespoon paprika |
| 2 | Teaspoons salt |
| ½ | each green and red peppers, slivered, for garnish. |

In bean-pot, in medium-high oven, heat butter, and then add marjoram, caraway seeds and lemon peel for 2 minutes. Stir in 2 cups of water, stew meat and remaining ingredients except peppers. Simmer, covered, 1½ hours or until fork-tender, stir occasionally. Pour into serving dish or in bean-pot; garnish with red and green pepper slivers.

Serves 6-8.

# Lamb Stew With Cornmeal Dumplings

| | |
|---|---|
| 2lbs. | Lamb stew meat, cut in 2 inch chunks |
| | All purpose flour |
| | Salad oil |
| 1 | Onion, quartered |
| 2 | Teaspoons salt |
| 1 | Teaspoon basil |
| ¼ | Teaspoon pepper |
| 2 | Cups diced celery |
| 4 | Whole carrots, diced |
| 10 | Small white onions |
| | Cornmeal Dumplings (below) |

**Prepare 2 hours before serving:**
On waxed paper, coat lamb with ¼ cup flour. In bean-pot heat 2 tablespoons hot salad oil, brown lamb in medium oven. Add 4 cups water, onion, salt, basil and pepper; simmer, covered, one hour. Add celery, carrots and onions and cook at high heat until mixture boils.

Meanwhile, prepare Cornmeal Dumplings (below). Drop dough by spoonfuls into boiling stew. Cook, uncovered on low heat for 10 minutes; cover and cook 10 minutes longer on low heat..

Cornmeal Dumplings: In medium bowl, with fork, lightly mix 1½ cups buttermilk biscuit mix, ½ cup yellow cornmeal and 2/3 cups milk.

Serves 6-8

# Vegetable Soup With Tiny Dumplings

| | |
|---|---|
| 2lbs. | Beef stew meat, cut in 1 inch chunks |
| 4 | Marrow bones |
| 1 | Medium onion |
| 2 | Whole cloves |
| 1 | Bay leaves |
| 4 | Teaspoons salt |
| 1 | Teaspoon chili powder |
| ¼ | Teaspoon pepper |
| 1 | 28 oz. can tomatoes |
| 1 | Cup chopped celery |
| 1 | Cup sliced carrots |
| ½ | Cup chopped parsnips |
| 1 | Tablespoon chopped parsley |
| | Tiny Dumplings (below) |

**Prepare 2 hours before serving.**
In covered bean-pot in high oven, heat stew meat, marrow bones and 6 cups hot water to boiling. Add onion, cloves, bay leaf, salt, chili powder and pepper. Lower heat to medium - low and simmer, covered 1 to 1½ hrs. until meat is almost tender.

Remove bones and take out marrow; set marrow aside. Skim any fat from surface. Return marrow to soup; add remaining ingredients except dumplings.

Cook, covered, on medium heat for 30 minutes or until meat is fork-tender. Meanwhile, prepare Tiny Dumplings; add them to soup and heat for 2 minutes. Makes 8-10 servings.

**Tiny Dumplings:**

In large bowl, combine 3 cups regular allpurpose flour, ½ teaspoon salt and ¼ teaspoon nutmeg. In small bowl, with fork, beat 4 eggs; beat eggs into flour mixture. Stirring constantly, pour 1 cup milk in then stream into flour mixture. Stir until dough is smooth. In large saucepan over high heat, heat 2 qts. water and ½ teaspoon salt to boiling. Over boiling water, press a little dough at a time through potato ricer or using back of wooden spoon, press dough through colander with large holes. Stir water gently so dumplings do not stick together. Boil 5 to 8 minutes until dumplings are tender.

# Barley Provencale

| | |
|---|---|
| 1 | Tablespoon olive oil |
| ½ | Large onion, chopped (about 3/4 cup) |
| 2 | Cloves garlic, minced |
| 3/4 | Cup pearl barley, rinsed and drained |
| 1¼ | Cups Chicken or vegetable broth |
| 1 | Large ripe tomato, peeled and diced, or |
| 1 | Cup canned crushed tomatoes |
| ¼ | Cup chopped fresh parsley |
| 1 | Tablespoon capers, rinsed and drained |
| | Salt and freshly ground black pepper to task. |

1.  Heat oil in a beanpot in medium high oven. Add onion and cook until translucent. Add garlic and barley and cook, stirring, until barley is lightly browned.

2.  Add broth, tomato, half the parsley, capers, salt and pepper. Bring to a boil, then cover, cook on low heat until liquid is absorbed, about 35 minutes. Add remaining parsley.

Serves 6

# Creamy Mushroom - Veal Stew

| | |
|---|---|
| 2½lbs. | Veal stew meat, cut in 1½ inch chunks |
| 1 | Carrot, diced |
| 7 | Medium onions, quartered |
| 2 | Teaspoons salt |
| 3 | Whole cloves |
| 1 | Bay leaf |
| 1lb. | Small mushrooms |
| 2 | Egg yolks |
| ½ | Cup whipping or heavy cream |
| 1 | Teaspoon lemon juice |
| | Chopped parsley for garnish |

## Prepare 3 hours before serving.

1.  In beanpot in medium high oven, heat to boiling 4 cups hot water, veal, carrot, one quartered onion, salt, cloves and bay leaf; reduce heat to low and simmer for about 1½ hours.

2.  With slotted spoon, remove veal to warm platter and set aside. With a fine sieve, strain broth; add remaining onions, cover and cook 10 minutes; add mushrooms and cook for 10 minutes or until onions are tender.

3.  With slotted spoon, remove onions and mushrooms; set asidewith veal. In high heat, cook broth to reduce it to 1/3 volume or about 1 2/3 cups. Return meat and vegetables to broth; heat.

4.  Meanwhile, in a small bowl, mix egg yolks, cream and lemon juice; stir in about ½ cup hot broth; stir mixture into stew. Heat until mixture thickens slightly. Sprinkle with parsley, if desired.

Serves 8

# Seafood Stew

| | |
|---|---|
| 1 | 16oz. pkg. frozen shrimp |
| 1 | 6oz. pkg. frozen king crab |
| 1 | 5oz. can oysters |
| ¼ | Cup salad oil |
| 3 | Tablespoons regular all—purpose flour |
| 2 | Medium onions, chopped |
| 1 | Garlic clove, chopped |
| 1 | 16oz. can tomatoes |
| 1 | Teaspoon chili powder |
| 1 | Teaspoon salt |
| ¼ | Teaspoon pepper |
| ¼ | Teaspoon hot pepper sauce |
| 2 | Tablespoons chopped parsley |
| 1 | Cup hot cooked rice cracked pepper |

**Prepare 30 minutes before serving.**
In beanpot, in medium oven, heat salad oil, stir in flour until blended. Stir in onions and garlic and cook until onions are tender. Stir in 3 cups water, tomatoes, chili powder, salt, pepper and hot pepper sauce. Cook, covered, 10 minutes. Stir in frozen shrimp, frozen crab, undrained oysters and parsley and cook 10 more minutes or until bubbly hot.

To serve, place a spoonful of hot, cooked rice into individual soup plates and spoon in stew. Serves 8.

Creole Stew: Prepare recipe above, but omit chili powder. At serving time, place 1 teaspoon chili powder in individual soup plates; add a spoonful of hot, cooked rice and spoon in seafood mixture, stirring until mixture thickens.

# Meatball Vegetable Soup

Meatballs:

| | |
|---|---|
| 1lb. | Ground beef |
| ¼ | Cup dried bread crumbs |
| ¼ | Cup tomato juice |
| 2 | Tablespoons instant minced onion |
| 2 | Teaspoons chili powder |
| 1½ | Teaspoons garlic salt |
| ¼ | Cup shortening |

Soup:

| | |
|---|---|
| 1 | 10 oz. can condensed beef broth |
| 1 | 10½ oz. can condensed vegetable soup |
| 1 | 10 oz. pkg. frozen lima beans |
| 1 | 16 oz. can tomatoes |
| 1/3 | Cup pkgd. precooked rice. |
| 1/3 | Cup grated carrots |
| 2 | Tablespoons instant minced onions |
| ¾ | Teaspoon salt |

**Prepare 45 minutes before serving.**
In large bowl, combine all ingredients for meatballs except short-ening; shape into 8 large balls. In medium skillet over medium heat, in melted shortening, brown meatballs. Cook, covered, over low heat 15 minutes.

Meanwhile, in beanpot in oven on high heat, cook undiluted beef broth, undiluted vegetable soup and lima beans 15 minutes; add remaining ingredients and meatballs and simmer 10 minutes.

Serves 5 to 6

# Fish Chowder

| | |
|---|---|
| 2 | 16 oz. pkgs. frozen flounder fillets, thawed |
| 4 | Large potatoes, sliced |
| 3 | Medium onions, sliced |
| 1 | Cup chopped celery |
| 1 | Garlic clove, minced |
| 4 | Whole cloves |
| 1 | Tablespoon salt |
| 1 | Bay leaf |
| ¼ | Teaspoon dill seed |
| ¼ | Teaspoon white pepper |
| 2 | Cups light cream or milk |
| ½ | Cup white wine |
| ¼ | Cup butter |

**Prepare 50 minutes before serving.**
In covered beanpot in medium oven, simmer potatoes, onions, celery, garlic, cloves, salt, bay leaf, dill seed, pepper and 1 cup water about 25 minutes, until tender.

Cut fish into large chunks. Add fish, 1 cup water and remaining ingredients to vegetables. Cook about 10 minutes, stirring occasionally, until bubbly hot.

Serves 8.

# Beef Cacciatore

| | |
|---|---|
| 3lbs. | Lean beef cut in 1 inch cubes |
| | Olive oil or salad oil |
| 2 | Medium onions chopped |
| | Flour |
| 2 | Medium cloves garlic, minced or mashed |
| 2 | Teaspoons salt |
| ½ | Teaspoon oregano |
| ½ | Teaspoon crushed red pepper or dash cayenne |
| 1 | Cup condensed consommé |
| ½ | Cup red wine |
| 1 lb. | Can whole tomatoes |
| 2 | Green peppers cut in strips |
| 12oz. | Noodles cooked |

1. Heat oil in heavy skillet and lightly brown onions. Remove them to a bowl for the moment.
2. Dredge the beef with flour and brown it well on all sides in thesame oil.
3. Transfer to beanpot and add to it the onions, garlic, salt, oregano, red pepper or cayenne, and consommé.
4. Cover and bake at 300° for 2 hours, or until beef is almost tender. Look at it occasionally and add a little consommé if it seems dry.
5. Add the wine and tomatoes, cover and bake 10 minutes more.
6. Stir in the green peppers and cook, uncovered, 15 minutes more.
7. Stir in cooked noodles.

Serves 8.

# Beef, Rice and Eggplant

| | |
|---|---|
| 1lb. | Lean ground beef |
| 1 | Medium eggplant cut in 1 inch cubes (unpeeled) |
| 2 | Cups cooked rice |
| 5 | Tablespoons salad oil |
| ½ | Cup minced onion |
| ¼ | Cup chopped green pepper |
| 1 | Tablespoon chopped parsley |
| 1 | Teaspoon salt |
| ¼ | Teaspoon pepper |
| ½ | Cup bread or corn flake crumbs |
| 2 | Tablespoons grated Parmesan cheese |

1. Cook the eggplant cubes in boiling salted water until tender, about 10 minutes. Drain well and wash.
2. Brown the beef in 3 tablespoons of the oil.
3. Add onion and green pepper and cook over low heat until onions are transparent.
4. Stir together the eggplant, meat mixture, parsley, salt, pepper, and rice. Turn into beanpot.
5. Stir the crumbs into the remaining 2 tablespoons oil and spread on top of the casserole.
6. Top with cheese and bake in a moderate oven, 375°, 20-25 minutes, or until brown and bubbling.

Serves 4-5

# Cassoulet

| | |
|---|---|
| 2 | Cups dried white beans |
| 8 | Slices bacon |
| ¼ | Cups diced salt pork |
| 1½ | lbs. pork loin cut into ¾ inch cubes |
| 1lb. | Lamb shoulder cut into ¾ inch cubes |
| 1 | Garlic sausage sliced |
| 1 | Carrot cut into ¼ inch slices |
| 1 | Onion stuck with 2 cloves |
| 3 | Cloves garlic cut in two |
| | Salt and pepper |
| 2 | Large onions, chopped |
| 2 | Tablespoons tomato paste |
| 3 | Cups beef buillion |
| 3 | Cups crumbs |

1. Soak beans in water to cover overnight, or at least 4 hrs., and drain.
2. Line beanpot with the bacon.
3. In a bowl, mix the beans, carrot, whole onion, 1 clove garlic, and salt and pepper to taste.
4. Pour this mixture into the pot, cover with water, and bake in a slow oven, 275°, 2 hrs.
5. While the beans are cooking, brown the meats in ¼ cup of the butter. Stir in the chopped onions, the 2 remaining garlic cloves, the tomato paste, and the boullion. Simmer over very low heat 1½ hrs., stirring occasionally.

6.  Turn the meat mixture into the beanpot, stir well, and top with one cup of the crumbs. Dot with ¼ cup of butter, increase the heat to 375°, and bake until the crumbs are brown, about 15 minutes.
7.  Stir the crumbs into the cassoulet and repeat this twice more, with the remaining crumbs. Serve when brown the third time.

Serves 6

Note: A duck or a chicken can be cut up, browned, and added if desired.

# Chicken Hotch Potch

| | |
|---|---|
| 1½lbs. | Chicken legs |
| 1 | Cup green peas |
| 1 | Cup lima beans |
| 2 | Carrots diced |
| 1 | Onion sliced |
| 1 | Small cauliflower broken into flowerets |
| 1 | Small head lettuce shredded |
| 2 | Tablespoons chopped parsley |

1.  Bring the chicken legs to a boil in the water, skimming the froth off as it forms. Put in bean pot both the chicken legs and the broth. Add the peas, beans, carrots, and onion. Cover and bake 1½ hrs. in slow oven, 325°.
2.  Add the cauliflower and lettuce and bake 35-40 minutes longer.
3.  Fish out the chicken legs, skin and bone them, and cut the meat into fair-sized chunks. Return to the "soup", add the parsley, and cook 10 minutes more. Check and correct seasoning.
4.  If you prefer this slightly thickened, stir in a flour-and-water paste.

For a little extra flavor, stir in ½ cup dairy sour cream too. Reheat and serve in large soup plates.

Serves 6

# Paella

| | |
|---|---|
| 4½ | lbs. chicken cut up |
| ½ | Cup olive oil (or salad oil) |
| 5 | Cloves garlic bruised but not peeled |
| 1 | Medium onion minced |
| 1 | Cup green beans cut up |
| 1 | Cup cauliflower flowerets |
| 1½ | Cups lobster, coarsely diced |
| 1½ | Cups shrimp, shelled and deveined |
| 2 | Medium tomatoes, chopped |
| 1½ | Teaspoons paprika |
| 3 | Cups dry rice (preferably wild, but then 2 cups) |
| 1 | Cup chopped parsley |
| | Salt |
| | Boiling water |

1. Heat the oil in a large heavy skillet and brown the garlic in it. Remove the garlic and brown the chicken pieces well. Arrange in beanpot.
2. Sauté the onion lightly in the skillet for 5 minutes.
3. At 5 minute intervals, add the following, in order: beans, cauliflower, lobster and shrimp together, tomatoes, paprika, rice, parsley.
4. When the parsley has been in 5 minutes, turn the whole mixture into the beanpot. Pour over boiling water barely to cover and bake, covered, 40 minutes in a slow oven, 300°. Check seasoning.

Serves 6-8

Note: If you use converted rice, add it dry - do not rinse. But if you use wild rice, wash it well in several waters.

# Rice And Sausage With Vegetables

| | |
|---|---|
| 3 | Cups cooked rice |
| ¾lb. | Sweet Italian sausages cut into ¼ inch slices |
| ¼ | Cup butter or margarine |
| 1 | Medium onion minced |
| 15oz. | Can artichoke hearts, drained and quartered |
| 1pkg. | Frozen peas, partly thawed |
| 3oz. | Can boiled, chopped mushrooms, drained |
| 1 | Can condensed consommé |
| ½ | Cup grated Parmesan cheese |

1.  Heat butter in a large, heavy skillet and lightly brown the onion   and sausage.
2.  Stir in the artichokes, peas, mushrooms, and ½ cup of the consommé. Simmer 10 minutes or so.
3.  Stir in rice and remaining consommé and pour into a greased medium beanpot.
4.  Sprinkle with cheese and bake 15 or 20 minutes in a moderate oven, 375°, or until cheese is well browned.

Serves 6

# Rice Hawaiian

| | |
|---|---|
| 2½ | Cups cooked rice |
| 3 | Tablespoons butter or margarine |
| 1 | Cup diced, cooked ham, chicken or tongue |
| ¾ | Cup diced pineapple, canned, fresh, or frozen. |
| ¼ | Cup pine nuts or slivered almonds |
| | Salt and pepper |
| ½ | Cup chopped watercress, stems removed |

Heat the butter in beanpot on low oven and lightly brown the ham. Add the pineapple, rice, nuts, and seasoning to taste. Cover and bake in oven at 350º, 15 minutes, or until piping hot. Sprinkle with watercress before serving.

Serves 4.

# Spaghetti Casserole Meal

| | |
|---|---|
| 1 | Cup thin spaghetti, broken up and cooked |
| 1 | Cup cooked turkey, chicken or diced roast meat |
| 1 | Cup julienned cooked ham |
| 1 | Cup diced sharp cheddar |
| 3 | Tablespoons butter or margarine |
| 2 | Tablespoons flour |
| 1 | Cup top milk |
| | Salt and pepper |
| 1 | Cup heavy cream |
| 1 | Bermuda onion sliced thin |
| | Paprika |

1. Make a cream sauce with the butter, flour, and milk, seasoning it to taste.
2. Stir into the sauce the meat and cheese, the well-drained spaghetti, and the cream. Pour into beanpot.
3. Top with layers of onion carefully arranged.
4. Sprinkle with paprika and bake 20 minutes in a slow oven, 325°.

Serves 6

# Peach-Rice Casserole Dessert

| | |
|---|---|
| 1 | Can sliced cling peaches (1lb. 13oz.), well drained |
| 2 | Cups cooked rice |
| ¼ | Cup sugar |
| ½ | Teaspoon salt |
| 2½ | Cups milk |
| 2 | Eggs |
| ½ | Teaspoon almond extract |
| 2 | Tablespoons brown sugar |

1.  Combine sugar, salt, milk, and eggs in top of double boiler and cook over hot, but not boiling, water, stirring almost constantly, about 20 minutes, until somewhat thickened.
2.  Remove from heat and add almond extract and rice.
3.  In a buttered beanpot, make alternate layers of peaches and rice.
4.  Top with brown sugar and bake about 30 minutes in moderate oven, 350°, or until the custard is set. Serve warm or cold, with cream or topped with a scoop of ice cream.

Serves 6.

# Quick Hot Spiced Fruit Casserole

| | |
|---|---|
| 1lb. | Can pineapple chunks |
| 1lb. | 14oz Can peach halves |
| 1lb. | 14oz. Can apricot halves |
| 1/3 | Cup melted butter |
| 2/3 | Cup brown sugar (packed) |
| ¼ | Teaspoon ground cloves |
| ¼ | Teaspoon cinnamon |
| 1 | Tablespoon curry powder or to taste |

Drain the fruits well and arrange in layers in beanpot. Combine the butter, sugar, and spices and sprinkle over the fruit. Bake 1 hour in a moderate over, 350°.

Serve hot with a scoop of ice cream on each serving.

Serves 8

# Maine Blueberry Pudding

| | |
|---|---|
| 2½ | Cups blueberries, washed and picked over |
| 1 | Cup sugar |
| 1/3 | Cup butter or margarine |
| 1 | Egg, well beaten |
| 1¼ | Cup flour |
| 2 | Teaspoons baking powder |
| ¼ | Teaspoon salt |
| 1/3 | Cup milk |
| ½ | Teaspoon vanilla |

1.  Cream ¾ cup of the sugar and the butter until fluffy and add thewell-beaten egg.
2.  Sift together flour, baking powder, and salt and add to the first mixture alternatively with the milk. Add vanilla.
3.  Carefully fold in 1½ cup of the blueberries, pour into a buttered beanpot, and bake about 45 minutes in a 350º oven, or until firm. The exact time will depend upon the thickness of the pudding in the beanpot.
4.  Mash the remaining cup of berries, add the remaining ¼ cup of sugar, and simmer 10 minutes over low heat. Strain and serve separately with the pudding, along with a pitcher of cream.

Serves 6

# Italienne Casserole

| | |
|---|---|
| 2lbs. | Ground beef |
| 2 | Medium onions, chopped |
| 1 | Clove garlic, crushed |
| 1 | Jar (14 oz.) spaghetti sauce |
| 1 | Can (16oz.) stewed tomatoes |
| 1 | Jar (3 oz.) mushrooms |
| 8oz. | Cooked macaroni shells |
| 2 | Cups sour cream |
| 1½ | lbs. provolone cheese |
| ½lb. | Mozarella cheese |

Brown ground beef, onions, and garlic in a large, heavy skillet. Combine spaghetti sauce, tomatoes, and mushrooms, and add to beef. Simmer, uncovered for 20 minutes.

Preheat oven to 350°.

Put ½ the cooked shells in beanpot and cover with ½ the meat sauce. Spread with ½ the sour cream and all the provolone cheese. Repeat with the remaining macaroni, meat sauce and sour cream; top with all of the mozzarella. Cover and bake for 35 minutes. Remove cover and bake for 10 to 15 minutes longer to brown.

Serves 8.

# Corned Beef in Casserole

| | |
|---|---|
| 6 | Tablespoons butter |
| 2 | Onions, finely chopped |
| 1 | Clove garlic, finely chopped |
| 1 | Green pepper, seeded and cut into thin strips |
| 2 | Cans (15oz. ea.) corned beef hash |
| 1 | Teaspoon dry mustard |
| 1 | Tablespoon Worcestershire sauce |
| 6 | Tablespoons chopped fresh parsley |
| | Buttered bread crumbs |
| | Grated cheese (Parmesan, Swiss or cheddar) |

Preheat oven to 400°.

Melt butter in skillet and sauté the onions, garlic and green pepper until soft. Add corned beef hash, dry mustard, and Worcestershire sauce. Place ½ of hash in buttered beanpot. Sprinkle with parsley and top with remaining hash. Top with buttered crumbs and grated cheese. Bake for 25-30 minutes until brown.

Serves 6.

# Baked Rice Pudding

½     Cup uncooked rice
4     Cups milk
½     Cup sugar
½     Teaspoon salt
1     Cup raisins
      Nutmeg

**Baking time 2½ hrs.**

Preheat oven to 275°. Grease beanpot. Measure ½ cup uncooked rice into strainer. Wash under running water. Shake strainer to drain off all water. Put rice into mixing bowl.

Add 4 cups milk (1 qt.). Add ½ cup sugar and ½ teaspoon salt. Stir the ingredients and pout into beanpot.

Bake in over for 1 hr. Pull it out and scatter 1 cup raisins over top of the pudding. Return pot to oven. Bake about 1½ hrs. longer or until a brown film covers the top of the pudding.

When done, take it out and sprinkle top lightly with nutmeg - enough to show speckles.

Chocolate lovers - may mix ¼ cup cocoa with the sugar when adding ingredients.

Serves 6

# Noodles With Mushrooms

| | |
|---|---|
| 8oz. | Pkg. medium noodles broken up and cooked |
| ½ | Cup sliced mushrooms or 4 oz. can drained |
| 1 | Medium onion, chopped |
| 1 | Small green pepper, chopped |
| ¼ | Cup chopped, stuffed olives |
| 3 | Tablespoons salad oil |
| 1 | Cup chicken broth |
| 1 | Cup condensed cream of mushroom soup |
| | Salt and pepper |
| 2 | Tablespoons grated Parmesan cheese |

1. Sauté the mushrooms, onion, pepper, and olives in oil.
2. Add chicken broth and soup and cook 2-3 minutes, stirring. Season.
3. Stir in cooked and well-drained noodles and pour into a greased beanpot.
4. Top with cheese and bake 25 min. at 325°.

Serves 4

## Macaroni With Wine

| | |
|---|---|
| 4 | Cups cooked macaroni |
| 1 | Medium onion, minced |
| 2 | Medium tomatoes, sliced |
| 2 | Tablespoons minced green pepper |
| 2 | Tablespoons butter |
| 2 | Hard-boiled eggs, diced |
| ½lb. | Sharp cheddar cheese, coarsely grated |
| ¼ | Cup dry sherry |

1. Melt butter in large skillet and cook the tomatoes, onion, and green pepper lightly, not browning them at all.
2. Gently stir in the eggs and macaroni and pour into a beanpot, well buttered.
3. In the top of a double boiler, over boiling water, melt the cheese, stirring occasionally.
4. When cheese is melted, blend in the sherry and pour over macaroni.
5. Bake at 350°, for 30 min.

Serves 4-5

# Mexican Macaroni

| | |
|---|---|
| 8oz. | Elbow macaroni, cooked barely tender |
| 1lb. | Pork sausage meat |
| ¾ | Cup chopped onion |
| ¾ | Cup chopped green pepper |
| 3 | Cups canned tomatoes, coarsely chopped |
| 2 | Cups dairy sour cream |
| 1 | Tablespoon sugar |
| 1 | Tablespoon chili powder |
| | Salt to taste |
| ¼ | Teaspoon dried oregano |

1. Cook sausage meat in heavy skillet, with the onion and green pepper, until the meat is somewhat browned, breaking up the sausage into small chunks. Drain off the fat.
2. Stir in tomatoes, sour cream, sugar, chili powder, salt, oregano, and well-drained macaroni.
3. Pour into beanpot, cover, and bake 35-40 min. at 375°, until macaroni is well done.
4. Remove cover last 10 min.

Serves 4

# Green Rice

| | |
|---|---|
| 2 | Cups cooked rice |
| 1 | Cup milk |
| 1 | Cup grated sharp cheddar cheese |
| ¼ | Cup butter, melted |
| 1 | Egg, well beaten |
| 2 | Tablespoons chopped onion |
| | Salt and pepper |
| 2/3 | Cup minced parsley, chopped spinach, chopped chives, or any combination of these. |

Combine all ingredients, with salt and pepper to taste, in well buttered beanpot. Bake 15 minutes at 350°.

Serves 5-6

# Creamy Turkey Soup

| | |
|---|---|
| 2 | Tablespoons butter |
| 1 | Large onion, minced |
| 2 | 13¾ oz. can chicken broth |
| 3 | Cups diced potatoes |
| 2 | Cups cubed, cooked turkey |
| 1 | 10oz. pkg. frozen peas and carrots |
| 2 | Teaspoons salt |
| ½ | Teaspoon pepper |
| 1/8 | Teaspoon rubbed sage |
| 1 | Cup light cream |
| 1 | Cup milk |

**Prepare 40 minutes before serving.**
In beanpot in medium high oven, in hot butter, cook onion until tender. Add chicken broth and potatoes and cook for 20 minutes. Stir in turkey, peas and carrots, salt, pepper and sage and cook 10 minutes or until vegetables are fork-tender. Stir in cream and milk and heat through.

Makes 10 cups or 6 servings.

# Frankfurter Chowder

| | |
|---|---|
| 2 | 16oz. pkgs. frankfurters, cut up |
| ¼ | Cup butter |
| 2 | Large onions, chopped |
| 1 | Stalk celery, chopped |
| 2 | Cups drained sauerkraut (1 16oz. can) |
| 1 | Bay leaf |
| ¼ | Teaspoon pepper |
| ¼ | Teaspoon thyme leaves |
| 2 | 13¾ oz. cans beef broth |
| 1½ | Cup sour cream |
| ½ | Cup chopped dill (optional) |

**Prepare 45 minutes before serving.**
In beanpot in high oven, in hot butter, cook onions, and celery until tender; stir in sauerkraut, bay leaf, pepper and thyme and cook 2 minutes. Add broth and simmer on medium low heat, covered about 15 minutes. Add frankfurters and cook 10 minutes longer. Serve topped with sour cream and dill.

Serves 6

# Catfish Stew

| | |
|---|---|
| 1 | 16oz. Pkg. frozen cod fillets, thawed and cut into chunks |
| 3 | Bacon slices, cut up |
| 1 | Onion, thinly sliced |
| 1 | 16 oz. can tomatoes |
| 1 | 16 oz. can potatoes, drained and halved |
| ¼ | Cup catsup |
| 1 | Teaspoon Worcestershire sauce |
| ¼ | Teaspoon seasoned pepper |
| 1/8 | Teaspoon thyme leaves |

**Prepare 40 minutes before serving.**
In beanpot in medium oven, cook bacon until just limp, add onion and cook until browned. Stir in remaining ingredients, except fish. Simmer 20 minutes. Add fillets and continue cooking 10 minutes longer.

Serves 4-5

# Winter Barley Soup

| | |
|---|---|
| 2½lbs. | Lamb stew meat, cut into 1½ inch chunks |
| 2 | Tablespoons butter |
| ½ | Cup barley |
| 2 | Medium onions sliced |
| 2 | Tablespoons chopped parsley |
| 2 | Teaspoons salt |
| ¼ | Teaspoon pepper |
| 1 | Bay leaf |
| 1½ | Cups chopped celery |
| 1½ | Cups sliced carrots |
| ½ | Medium green pepper, diced |
| ¼ | Teaspoon thyme leaves |

**Prepare 2½ hrs. before serving.**
In beanpot in medium-high oven, brown lamb in butter; add 6 cups hot water and next 6 ingredients. Simmer, covered on medium-low heat about 1½ hrs. Stir in remaining sliced onion and the rest of ingredients and cook 30 minutes or until meat is tender. Remove bay leaf.

Serves 8

# Baked Beans With Maple Sugar

| | |
|---|---|
| 2 | Cups yellow eye beans |
| ½ | Teaspoon baking soda |
| ½lb. | Heavy bacon |
| 8-10 | Tablespoons maple sugar |
| 4 | Cups boiling water |
| 2 | Teaspoons salt |
| 1 | Medium sliced onion |

1. Soak yellow eye beans overnight.
2. Drain, and boil with ½ teaspoon baking soda.
3. And then simmer slowly until skins burst.
4. Drain, place in tightly covered beanpot with ½ lb. heavy bacon, 8-10 tablespoons maple sugar, 4 cups boiling water, 2 teaspoons salt, 1 medium sliced onion.

**Bake for 5 hours or more.**

# Casserole of Beans

| | |
|---|---|
| 1lb. | Dried pea beans or |
| 1 | Large can baked beans |
| 1 | Teaspoon salt |
| ¼ | Teaspoon pepper |
| 2 | Tablespoons brown sugar |
| 1 | Small can tomatoes |
| 1 | Medium-sized onion |
| 4 | Slices bacon, chopped |

1. If dried beans are used, soak overnight; drain off the water; and cook tender in salted boiling water.
2. Season the beans with the salt, pepper and sugar; and arrange alternate layers of the prepared beans and tomatoes in a beanpot, finishing with tomatoes.
3. Peel and slice the onion; arrange on top; and sprinkle with the chopped bacon.
4. Cover; and bake in a slow oven for one hour. Then remove thecover; and continue baking until the beans have absorbed most of the moisture.

# Baked Lima Beans

| | |
|---|---|
| 1 lb. | Large lima beans, dried |
| 1 | Small onion, chopped |
| 1/3 | Cup brown sugar |
| ½ | Cup ketchup |
| 2 | Tablespoon unsulphured molasses |
| | Salt and pepper to taste |
| ½ lb. | Bacon |

1. Soak beans overnight in 1 teaspoon salt.
2. Cook lima beans until tender. Drain but save juice and put beans in beanpot.
3. Mix all ingredients except bacon. Pour over beans and put enough juice until you can see it at the top of the beans.
4. Cut strips of bacon into 1" pieces and lay on top of beans.
5. Bake at 350° for 1 hour uncovered.

Serves 5-6

# Baked Beans Michigan Style

| | |
|---|---|
| 1 | Pint pea beans |
| 2 | Onions |
| ½ | Cup sour cream |
| 1½ | Teaspoons salt |
| ½ | Teaspoon pepper |
| 1 | Tablespoon molasses |

1. Soak the beans overnight. Drain, and rinse.
2. Bring to a boil in water to cover, containing one third tea spoon  baking soda.
3. Drain, and combine with the onions, chopped, the cream and seasonings in a beanpot.
4. Barely cover with boiling water; and bake until tender, about three hours. Then uncover to brown.

# New England Baked Bean Pot

| | |
|---|---|
| 1lb. | Navy beans |
| 2 | Teaspoons salt |
| 1 | Teaspoon dry mustard |
| ½ | Teaspoon pepper |
| 1 | Cup chopped onion |
| ½ | Cup maple syrup |
| ¼ | Cup cider vinegar |
| ½lb. | Salt pork, cubed |

1. Soak beans in water overnight. Drain.
2. Pour into beanpot with seasonings, onion, maple syrup, cider vinegar, and salt pork.
3. Cover and bake at 300° for 6 hrs. Uncover last half hour to brown beans.

# Easy Baked Beans

| | |
|---|---|
| 4 | Slices bacon |
| ½ | Cup chopped onion |
| 2 | 1 lb. cans (4 cups) pork and beans with tomato sauce |
| 2 | Tablespoons brown sugar |
| 1 | Tablespoon Worcestershire sauce |
| 1 | Teaspoon prepared mustard |

1. Cook bacon until crisp; drain reserving 2 tablespoons drippings. Crumble bacon.
2. Cook onion in reserved drippings until tender but not brown; add with crumbled bacon to remaining ingredients, mixing well.
3. Turn into beanpot. Bake uncovered at 350° about 2 hours.

Serves 6.

# Chicken Casserole

| | |
|---|---|
| 1 | Chicken (2½ lbs.) |
| 1½ | Tablespoons olive oil |
| 4 | Tablespoons butter |
| 1 | Medium onion, finely chopped |
| 1 | Stalk celery |
| 1 | Carrot, finely chopped |
| 1 | 14 oz. can peeled tomatoes, squeeze and break into small pieces |
| ½ | Cup dry white wine |
| 2 | Whole cloves |
| 1 | Pinch cinnamon |
| 1lb. | Whole mushrooms |

1. Wash chicken and cut into bite-size pieces.
2. Heat oil and butter in beanpot. Put in oven on low heat. Saute onion, carrot, and celery. Add the chicken and fry until it is golden brown.
3. Raise the heat and add tomatoes. Cook for 5 minutes, stirring frequently. Add white wine and let come to a boil, stir well. Now add the cloves and cinnamon and lower the heat. Continue cooking until the chicken is tender, about ½ hr., stir once or twice.
4. Fifteen minutes before the chicken is cooked, add the whole mushrooms. Season with salt and pepper.
5. Let sit for 20 minutes before serving.

# Lima Bean and Tomato Casserole

4 Cups boiled, dried lima beans
1 No. 2 can (or 2½ cups cooked) tomatoes
¾ Teaspoon salt
 Few grains pepper
½ Teaspoon sugar
2 Bay leaves
6 Thin slices cooked ham

1. Combine beans, tomatoes, salt, pepper, sugar and bay leaves.
2. Pour into greased beanpot; top with ham. Bake in moderate oven (350°) 30 minutes.

Serves 4

# Baked Bean Soup - I

| | |
|---|---|
| 3 | Cups baked beans |
| 1qt. | Water or stock |
| 2 | Tablespoons minced onion |
| 2-3 | Tablespoons finely chopped celery |
| 4 | Uncooked franks, or ¼ cup diced salt pork or hard sausage |
| 1 | Teaspoon instant coffee (optional) |
| 2 | Tablespoons sherry |
| 1 | Lemon, sliced |
| 2 | Eggs, hard-boiled and finely chopped |

1. Combine beans, water or stock, onion, and celery, divide into 3 or 4 batches, and spin each batch in a blender until smooth.
2. Let this resulting puree´ simmer in oven on low heat for about 30 minutes, adding a little liquid only if it seems too thick. (One Vermont cook adds a teaspoon of instant coffee to give her soup a deeper color; the flavor blends into the point of mystery).
3. Cook franks or fry salt pork until crisp; if using sausage, cut into small dice. Add meat to soup and continue to heat in oven at 350º.
4. Add sherry just before ladling soup into hot dishes. Put a lemon  slice in each serving and sprinkle in bits of chopped egg.

Serves 6

# Baked Bean Soup - II

| | |
|---|---|
| 2 | Cups cold baked beans |
| 2 | Medium-sized onions, minced |
| ½ | Clove garlic, finely chopped |
| 4 | Cups cold water |
| 2 | Cups canned tomatoes |
| 2 | Tablespoons flour |
| 2 | Tablespoons butter |
| | Salt and freshly ground black pepper to taste |

1. Place the beans, onions, garlic and water in a beanpot and simmer in a low oven for about 30 minutes.
2. Heat the tomatoes, put through an electric blender or food mill and add to the bean mixture.
3. Mix the flour and butter together and add a little of the hot soup. Return all to the pot and cook, stirring occasionally, until soup thickens. Season with salt and pepper.

Serves 6

# Baked Bean Soup - III

| | |
|---|---|
| 3 | Cups cold baked beans |
| 3 | Pints water |
| 2 | Small onions, sliced |
| 2 | Stalks celery |
| 1½ | Cups stewed and strained tomatoes |
| 2 | Tablespoons butter |
| 2 | Tablespoons flour |
| 1 | Tablespoon chili sauce |
| | Salt and pepper |

1. Put the first 4 ingredients into a beanpot. Simmer for 30 minutes in a low oven.
2. Rub through a sieve, add tomato and chili sauce, season to taste with salt and pepper, and bind with butter and flour cooked together.

# Beatnik Baked Beans

| | |
|---|---|
| 2 | Cups pea beans |
| 1/3 | Cup sorghum |
| 1 | Onion |
| 1 | Cup tomatoes,fresh or stewed |
| 1 | Teaspoon salt |
| 1 | Teaspoon dry mustard |
| 1/8 | Teaspoon garlic salt |
| 4 | Tablespoons oil |

1. Soak beans overnight and cook until tender.
2. Add the remaining ingredients. Mix well. Bake in covered beanpot for 3 hours in a slow oven. Uncover for last hour.

# Baked Beans With No Molasses

| | |
|---|---|
| 1 | Cup dried pea (navy) beans, water to cover |
| 1 | Medium onion, chopped fine |
| 1 | Teaspoon salt |
| 1 | Teaspoon dry mustard |
| ½ | Box (1 firmly packed cup) dark brown sugar |
| ¼lb. | Salt pork scored on one side |
| ½ | Cup ketchup |

1. Wash and sort beans. Soak overnight in water to cover.
2. In the morning, drain and add fresh water. Cover and simmer until soft; about 30 to 40 minutes.
3. Pour into a beanpot; add just enough water to cover beans; then stir in all the remaining ingredients.
4. Cover and bake at 300° for 5 to 7 hours. Uncover the last hour to let liquid thicken.

Serves 8.

# Netta's Southern Baked Beans

| | |
|---|---|
| 1 | Small green pepper |
| 1 | Small onion |
| 1 | Fresh tomato |
| ½ | Teaspoon of each: freshly ground pepper, dry mustard, and paprika |
| 1½ | Tablespoons dark corn syrup |
| 1 | Tablespoon Worcestershire sauce |
| 1 | Can (28 oz.) pork and beans |

1. Seed and chop green pepper. Chop onion; peel and chop tomato.
2. Mix pepper, mustard, and paprika with corn syrup and Worcestershire sauce.
3. Combine all ingredients with beans and spoon into a beanpot. Bake at 300° for 1 hour.

Serves 4-6

* Prepare in advance, refrigerate, and bake when needed.

# Bourbon Baked Beans

| | |
|---|---|
| 4 | Cans (13 oz. ea.) baked beans |
| 4 | Oranges, thinly sliced |
| 1 | Lemon, thinly sliced |
| 1 | Cup raisins |
| 1 | Cup molasses |
| ¼ | Teaspoon ground ginger |
| ½ | Cup bourbon |

1. Combine all ingredients except bourbon.
2. Put into a beanpot.
3. Gradually add bourbon and carefully mix to blend.
4. Bake at 300° for 45 to 50 minutes.

Serves 8

* Serve with sliced baked ham, a sturdy salad and hot rolls.

# Baked Lima Beans With Gingersnaps

2      Packages (10 oz. each) frozen lima beans, thawed
1      Cup sour cream
2      Tablespoons brown sugar
1      Tablespoon grainy mustard
       Dash Worcestershire sauce
1¼    Cup crushed gingersnaps
4      Tablespoons (½ stick) unsalted butter, melted

1. Preheat oven to 350°.
2. Place the lima beans in beanpot. Mix the sour cream, brown sugar, mustard, and Worcestershire sauce and stir into the lima beans. Combine the gingersnaps and butter and sprinkle evenly over the beans.
3. Bake uncovered for 45 minutes. Serve hot.

Serves 6-8

# Baked Rice & Beans

3      Slices bacon, cut in ½
½      Cup chopped onion
6      Tablespoons ketchup
2      Tablespoons brown sugar
1      Teaspoon Dijon-style mustard
½      Teaspoon salt
       Freshly ground pepper to taste
1½     Cups cooked rice
1      Can (15 oz.) pinto beans

1.   In a 10 inch skillet, cook bacon until about ½ done. Remove bacon. Add onions to skillet and cook until soft but not browned.
2.   Mix in remaining ingredients.
3.   Spoon into a buttered bean pot.
4.   Arrange bacon strips on top.
5.   Bake uncovered at 350º for 30 to 35 minutes.

Makes 4 servings

* Sautéed cherry tomatoes, spinach salad, and rye bread could finish the menu.

# Sister Josephine's Shaker Baked Beans

| | |
|---|---|
| 4 | Cups dried pea beans or navy beans |
| 1 | Onion |
| ½ | Cup unsulphered molasses |
| ½ | Cup butter |
| 1 | Teaspoon salt |
| 2 | Teaspoons dry mustard |
| ½ | Cup ketchup |

1.  Day before, pick over and wash beans, cover beans with water and soak overnight. Next day, drain beans and add two and one half cups hot water. Cook until tender, about 45 minutes.
2.  Preheat oven to 350°.
3.  Place the onion in the bottom of a well-buttered beanpot. Drain beans and save the liquid. Pour beans into beanpot.
4.  Add the remaining ingredients to the reserved bean liquid and pour over beans to cover. Cover pot and cook 2½ hours, adding more liquid whenever necessary. Remove cover and bake a ½ hour longer to brown well.

Serves 10-12

# Maine Home-Baked Beans

| | |
|---|---|
| 2lbs. | Dried pea beans or navy beans |
| | Water |
| ¾lb. | Salt pork |
| 1 | Onion |
| 2/3 | Cup unsulphered molasses |
| 1 | Teaspoon dry mustard |
| 1½ | Teaspoons salt |
| | Boiling water |

1. Day before, pick over the beans and wash well. Place in a bowl and cover with cold water so that the water extends 2 inches above the beans. Soak overnight. Next morning put beans and soaking water in a heavy pot.
2. Make ½ inch deep cuts through the rind of the salt pork at ½ inch intervals, add to beans. Bring to a boil and simmer them until the skin cracks when a bean is held in the hand and blown on, about 1 hour.
3. Preheat oven to 250°.
4. Place the onion in the bottom of a beanpot. Add the beans, cube the salt pork and add.
5. Stir in the remaining ingredients, including enough boiling water to cover beans. Baked uncovered, 6 to 8 hours, stirring occasionally and adding more boiling water when ever necessary so that beans are always just submerged.

Serves 10-12

* To prepare Vermont baked beans, substitute maple syrup or honey for the molasses in the recipe above.

## Baked Beans - I

| | |
|---|---|
| 1lb. | Dried pea beans or navy beans |
| 1 | Bay leaf |
| 1 | Celery rib, halved |
| 3 | Sprigs parsley |
| 1 | Sprig fresh thyme or ½ teaspoon dried thyme |
| ½lb. | Salt pork |
| 2/3 | Cup unsulphured molasses |
| ¼ | Cup brown sugar |
| 2 | Teaspoons dry mustard |
| 2 | Teaspoons salt |
| ¼ | Teaspoon freshly ground black pepper |
| 1 | Medium-sized onion, coarsely chopped |
| 1 | Cup sherry |

1. Soak the beans overnight in cold water to cover.
2. Next day, drain beans; then cover with fresh water. Tie the bay leaf, celery, parsley and thyme in a bundle. Add to kettle. Bring to a boil and simmer slowly until beans skins blow off when blown upon lightly, 30 to 60 minutes.
3. Drain beans, reserving 2 qts. of the cooking liquid. Slice the salt pork into ¼ inch slices. Arrange the beans and ½ the sliced pork in alternative layers in a beanpot, score the remaining pork and place in the top layer of beans.
4. Preheat oven to 300°.
5. Combine the molasses, brown sugar, mustard, salt, pepper, onion, and reserved cooking liquid. Pour over the beans. Bake, covered, 6 to 8 hours. 1 hour before beans are to be done, pour the sherry over them. Replace cover and bake 1hour longer.

Serves 6-8

# Baked Beans - II

½lb.    Salt pork, cut into squares
1lb.    Dried white Michigan or pea beans
½      Cup brown sugar
½      Cup unsulphured molasses
1      Teaspoon dry mustard
1      Teaspoon salt
1      Onion, studded with 2 whole cloves

1. Day before, place the salt pork and beans in a large mixing bowl and add water to cover to the depth of one inch. Let stand overnight.
2. Next day, drain beans and pork and pour into a sauce pan. Add the remaining ingredients and water to barely cover, and bring to a boil. Simmer, partially covered, 1 hour.
3. Preheat oven to 350°.
4. Discard the onion and pour the beans into beanpot. Cover and bake 2½ hours. Look at beans occasionally and, if they are cooking too fast, reduce the oven heat.They should bubble nicely.

Serves 6

# Connecticut Beanpot

| | |
|---|---|
| 1 lb. | Italian hot sausages, sliced Serves 10-12 |
| 1 lb. | Italian sweet sausages, sliced |
| 1 | Kielbasa (Polish sausage), sliced |
| 3 | Onions, sliced and separated into rings |
| ½ | Teaspoon thyme |
| ½ | Teaspoon basil |
| 2 | Bay leaves |
| ¾ | Cup dry sherry |
| 3 | 1 lb. cans pork and beans |
| 1 | 8 oz. can tomato sauce |
| | Whole or sliced frankfurters (optional) |

1. Preheat the oven to 350º.
2. Place the sausages and onions in beanpot and cook gently until sausages are done.
3. Add the remaining ingredients and bring to a boil. Cover and bake 1½ hours. If desired, frankfurters, whole or sliced, may be added during the last 20 minutes of baking.

# Monday's Beanpot Stew

| | |
|---|---|
| 2 | Tablespoons bacon drippings |
| 1lb. | Top round beef, cut into cubes |
| 2 | Onions, sliced |
| 3 | Carrots, sliced |
| 1 | White turnip, diced |
| ¼ | Yellow turnip, diced |
| 2 | Ribs celery, diced |
| | Salt and fresh ground pepper to taste |
| ¼ | Cup old-fashioned oats |
| | Boiling Water |
| 3 | Potatoes, cubed |

1. Preheat the oven to 350°.
2. Heat the bacon drippings in a skillet, add the beef cubes and brown all sides. Add the onions, carrots, white turnip, yellow turnip, celery, salt and pepper. Turn into a beanpot.
3. Stir in the oats and enough boiling water barely to cover. Bake 2 hours, replenishing water as needed. Add the potatoes and cook one hour longer.

Serves 4

## Grandfather's Baked Beans and Duck

| | |
|---|---|
| ½lb. | Dried pea beans |
| 3 | Cups beer |
| 1 | Cup beef stock |
| 1 | Bay leaf |
| 1 | Small-size onion, chopped |
| ½ | Lemon, chopped |
| 1 | Tablespoon maple sugar |
| ¼ | Cup unsulphured blackstrap molasses |
| 1 | Tablespoon Worcestershire sauce |
| ½ | Tablespoon Dijon mustard |
| ¼ | Teaspoon ground cumin seed |
| ½ | Teaspoon ground savory |
| | Freshly ground pepper to taste |
| ½ | Cup diced salt pork |
| 1 | Duck (3-4 lbs.) |
| ¼ | Cup water |
| ¼ | Cup chopped, candied ginger root |

1. Preheat oven to 350º.
2. Soak beans in 2 cups beer overnight.
3. Mix remaining 1 cup beer with stock, combine with beans soaked in beer, and pour all into beanpot.
4. Add bay leaf, onion, ginger root, lemon, maple sugar, molasses, seasonings, and salt pork.
5. Cover and bring to a boil, then put beanpot in oven and bake for 3 hours, adding a little water every 30 minutes as necessary; there should be enough liquid to cover beans by 1 inch.

6.  Cut duck into 4 or 6 pieces, pulling fat away from meat. Render fat in a skillet large enough to hold all of duck pieces flat. Brown the pieces for 8 to 10 minutes, turning often so that all surfaces are seared; when browned, transfer to beanpot and push down into beans and liquid.

7.  Pour off duck fat from skillet and stir in water, scraping up brown bits on bottom of pan and letting liquid sizzle for about 1 minute; pour over duck and beans in beanpot. Cover and continue baking for 3 to 4 hours, checking occasionally and adding water, if necessary, to keep beans covered. When done, they will have absorbed most of the liquid, including any fat that may still come from duck; the meat should be falling off the bones.

Serves 3-5

# Border Beans

| 3 | Cups dried pinto beans |
|---|---|
| 8 | Cups vegetable or soybean broth |
| 5 | Cloves garlic, chopped |
| 1-3 | Dried red chiles, crumbled |
| 2 | Teaspoons dried oregano |
| | A few dashes of liquid smoke |

1. Soak beans in water to cover for 8 hours.
2. Discard the water and place the soaked beans in a beanpot with remaining ingredients.
3. Place in oven at 350°. Bring to a boil, simmer for about 3 minutes, then turn the heat to low, cover, and simmer for 2-3 hours, or until the beans are very tender. The beans should be a bit "soupy" (the broth is delicious). If you have used a salt-free or low salt broth, adjust for salt now.

Serves 6-8

# Baked Beans With Black Duck Breasts And Linguica Sausages

| | |
|---|---|
| 2lbs. | Dried navy, cranberry, or Yellow eye beans |
| 1lb. | Salt pork with skin attached |
| 2 | Tablespoons dry mustard |
| 1 | Teaspoon cider vinegar |
| ¼ | Cup dark rum |
| ½ | Cup molasses |
| 1 | Teaspoon salt (optional) |
| 1 | Medium-large onion, studded with 12 cloves |
| 3 | Linguica sausages |
| ¾lb. | Lean pork fat, cut into ¼ inch cubes |
| 6 | Boneless, skinless Black Duck breasts (also called Canadian Redleg) or substitute Mallard or Muscovy duck breasts |
| | Salt and freshly milled pepper |
| ½lb. | Unsalted butter |
| | Small bunch fresh sage |

1. Thoroughly wash and pick over the beans. Place in a pot with plenty of water and set aside to soak overnight.
2. Drain the beans, place them in a large kettle and add cold water to cover. Bring to a boil over high heat. Reduce the heat to low and simmer for 30 minutes. Drain beans and reserve the cooking liquid.
3. Preheat the oven to 200º.
4. Cut away the salt pork skin in one sheet. Line the beanpot with the skin, skin side up.

5.  In a small bowl, combine the dry mustard, vinegar, rum, molasses, and salt. Mix into the beans and fill the beanpot one-third full with the bean mixture. Add the clove-studded onion and top with more beans and salt pork. Cover with the remaining beans. Cover the beanpot and bake for 10 to 11 hours, checking the liquid from time to time. If the beans begin to dry out, add some of the reserved bean liquid to moisten them. Uncover the beans for the last hour of cooking and bury the linguica sausages in the beans. About 30 minutes before serving, render the cubed pork fat over moderately low heat until golden, draining off the fat as it cooks. Drain the cubes on paper towels and set aside in a warm place.

**The duck breasts:**

6.  Lightly season the duck breasts with salt and pepper. Warm the butter in a large ovenproof skillet set over moderately high heat. Add some of the sage leaves and sauté' the breasts for 2 minutes on each side, until rare. Place the skillet in the oven for 3 to 4 minutes while you assemble the dish.

**To assemble:**

7.  Remove the onion from the beans and discard it. Remove the sausage from the beans. Peel off the skin and slice ¼ inch thick. Arrange the sliced sausages in the center of a warm platter. Surround the sausages with the duck breasts and place one or two whole sage leaves over each breast. Sprinkle with the reserved rendered pork fat. Serve with the beans.

Serves 6 to 8

Note: If the salt pork is very salty, boil it first. Otherwise it will burn and brown before the fat is rendered.

# Haitian Baked Beans

| 1 lb. | Dry white beans |
|---|---|
| 2 | Teaspoons butter |
| 1 | Clove garlic, bruised |
| 1 | Large onion, finely chopped |
| 3 | Strips crisply fried bacon, crumbled |
| 2 | Tablespoons dark brown sugar |
| 2 | Teaspoons Worcestershire sauce |
| 4 | Tablespoons molasses |
| 5 | Tablespoons chili sauce |
| 1 | Tablespoon dry English mustard |
| 1 | Teaspoon curry powder |
| 1½ | Teaspoons salt |
| ½ | Cup dark rum |
| 1½ | Cups tomato juice (approximately) |
| 3 | Strips uncooked bacon |

1. Place beans in a large pot of boiling water and return to boiling. Turn off heat; let stand 1 hour. Heat oven to 275°.
2. Grease a beanpot with butter; rub with garlic. Drain beans; place in a mixing bowl. Add all ingredients through rum, mix well. Add ¼ cup tomato juice; transfer to beanpot. Place uncooked bacon on top. Bake covered 7 or more hours, adding tomato juice as beans dry out.

# Eastern Baked Beans

| | |
|---|---|
| 2 | Cups small white navy or pea beans |
| 6 | Cups water |
| 2 | Tablespoons sesame meal* |
| 1 | Small onion, peeled and whole |
| 1 | Cup reserved bean liquid |
| ¾ | Cup fancy molasses or ½ cup honey or other liquid sweetener and ¼ cup blackstrap molasses |
| 2 | Teaspoons salt |
| 1 | Teaspoon dry mustard |
| | Remaining bean liquid |

1. Soak beans in water to cover for 8 hours. Drain off the soaking water, and bring the soaked beans to a boil in a large pot with 6 cups water.
2. Lower the heat and simmer the beans for 10 minutes. Drain the beans and reserve the cooking water. Preheat the oven to 300°. Place beans in beanpot and mix with the sesame meal.
3. Insert onion into the center of the beans.
4. Combine 1 cup reserved bean liquid, fancy molasses, salt and dry mustard, and pour over the beans, stirring well. Add just enough reserved bean liquid to cover the beans. Cover the pot and bake for 2 hours. Add remaining bean liquid.
5. Stir well and bake for 1½ to 2 hours more, or until the beans are very tender and the liquid is absorbed. Bake uncovered for the last half hour.

Serves 6

# * Sesame Meal (makes a generous 2 cups)

2      Cups hulled, raw sesame seeds.

1.    Place sesame seeds in a heavy, dry skillet over high heat.
2.    Stir constantly until the seeds turn golden-beige and start to pop. Remove from the heat and cool slightly. Pour the seeds into a blender, and blend at high speed, stopping and stirring from the bottom a few times, until the consistency of fine meal (but not a paste). Keep in a covered container in the freezer to store.

# New Orleans Style Red Beans

| | |
|---|---|
| 1lb. | Small dried red beans (not kidney beans) |
| 2 | Cups onions, minced |
| 6 | Green onions, chopped |
| 1 | Green bell pepper, seeded and chopped |
| 1 | Cup fresh parsley, chopped |
| 1 | Stalk celery, chopped |
| 4 | Cloves garlic, chopped |
| ½ | Cup tomato paste |
| 1 | Large bay leaf |
| 2-3 | Tablespoons soy sauce |
| 1½ | Teaspoons ground coriander |
| 1 | Teaspoon ground cumin |
| ½ | Teaspoon of each: ground tumeric, dried oregano, dried thyme, and liquid smoke, pinch of cayenne pepper |

1. Soak beans in water to cover for at least 8 hours.
2. Drain and rinse. Place the beans in beanpot with enough water to cover with remaining ingredients.
3. Put in oven at 350°. Bring to a boil, simmer for 3 minutes, reduce heat to low, cover, and simmer for about 2 hours, or until the beans are soft and the liquid is "creamy". Taste and adjust for salt, pepper and liquid smoke. Serve over steamed rice with cooked greens and Louisiana-style liquid hot sauce on the side.

# Fruited Baked Beans With Chutney

| | |
|---|---|
| 2 | Cups dried navy beans or soybeans, washed |
| 1qt. | Water |
| 1½ | Teaspoons salt, preferably sea salt, or to taste |
| 1½ | Teaspoons dry mustard |
| 1 | Onion, chopped fine |
| ½ | Cup chutney, minced |
| | Freshly ground pepper |
| 2 | Apples, sliced |
| 3 | Peaches (in season) peeled and sliced |
| ½ | Cup dried apricots |
| ¼-½ | Cup mild honey, or to taste |
| ¼ | Cup molasses |
| ½ | Cup plain yogurt |

1. Soak beans overnight, or for at least several hours. Cook in the soaking liquid with 1 teaspoon salt for about 1 hour, until tender but not mushy. Drain, reserving 1 cup of the liquid.
2. In a small bowl, dissolve the mustard in the bean liquid and combine with the finely chopped onion, the chutney, and salt and pepper to taste. Stir this into the beans.
3. Preheat the oven to 325°; oil the beanpot. Pour half of the bean mixture into the prepared beanpot. Top with a layer of sliced apples, peaches, and apricots, then pour in the rest of the bean mixture and top with the rest of the fruit. Combine the honey and molasses and pour evenly over the top.

4.     Cover and bake for 1 hour, then remove the cover and bake for another 30 minutes. About 5 minutes before removing from the oven, pour on the yogurt. Serve steaming hot, with corn bread or brown rice.

Serves 6-8

# Beef And Three Bean Casserole

| | |
|---|---|
| 8oz. | Lean ground beef |
| 2 | Cups cooked or canned drained chickpeas (ceci or garbanzo beans) |
| 1 | Cup cooked or canned, drained kidney beans |
| 1 | Cup chopped onions |
| ½ | Cup spicy tomato juice |
| 2 | Tablespoons chili sauce |
| 1 | Tablespoon prepared mustard |
| 1 | Tablespoon wine vinegar |
| 1 | Clove garlic, minced |
| ½ | Teaspoon dried oregano |
| 1 | Cup frozen kitchen-cut green beans |

1. Brown the beef with no fat added in a non-stick skillet or under the broiler. Drain and discard any fat.
2. In beanpot, combine browned beef with all remaining ingredients except green beans, cover, and bake for 1 hour in a preheated 325° oven.
3. Meanwhile, partially thaw green beans. Arrange green beans on top of mixture; cook, uncovered, just until green beans are hated through but still bright green and crunchy - 6-8 minutes. Stir into mixture and serve immediately.

Serves 4

# Lentils, Tuscany Style

| | |
|---|---|
| 8oz. | Low-calorie breakfast sausage |
| 1 | Large sweet onion, chopped |
| 2½ | Cups water or fat skimmed broth |
| 2 | Tablespoons chopped celery |
| 2 | Tablespoons chopped parsley |
| 2 | Bay leaves |
| 1 | Cup dried lentils, picked over and rinsed |
| | Salt or lemon pepper to taste (optional) |

1. Brown sausages under broiler; discard fat.
2. Combine all ingredients in covered beanpot and bake in preheated 350° oven for 40 to 50 minutes or until lentils are tender  but not mushy. Remove bay leaves before serving.

Serves 6

# Boston Brown Beans

| ½lb. | Tofu |
|------|------|
| 1 | Cup cabbage |
| ½ | Cup oil |
| 3 | Cups dried navy pea or lima beans |
| 1 | Cup water |
| ½ | Cup tomato puree |
| 1 | Tablespoon salt |
| 1 | Cup molasses |
| 2 | Tablespoons mustard powder |

1. Soak beans in water overnight. Then drain.
2. Sauté cabbage and tofu in oil until tender.
3. Combine with remaining ingredients and bake in beanpot, covered, in oven at 250° for 1-1½ hours or until tender.

Add more liquid as needed.

# Smoked Turkey, Black-Eyed Peas, and Rice

| | |
|---|---|
| 1 | Smoked turkey drumstick |
| 1lb. | Black-eyed peas, fresh or frozen and thawed |
| 1 | Cup uncooked brown rice |
| 4 | Onions, chopped |
| 4 | Ribs celery, sliced |
| 1 | Green bell pepper, seeded and chopped |
| 1 | Cup tomato juice |
| 1 | Cup dry red wine |
| 1 | Cup water |
| 4 | Cloves garlic, minced |
| 1 | Teaspoon of each; dried rosemary, sage, and thyme |
| 2-3 | Bay leaves |
| | Salt and black pepper to taste |

1. Combine ingredients in a beanpot. Cover and bake in a 350° degree oven for 2 hours.
2. Discard bone and skin from turkey leg; cut meat into bite size chunks. Stir turkey meat back into rice mixture. Remove bay leaves before serving.

Serves 8

# Indian Pudding

| | |
|---|---|
| 1½ | Quarts milk |
| ½ | Cup yellow corn meal |
| ¾ | Cup molasses |
| 6 | Tablespoons sugar |
| ¾ | Teaspoon salt |
| 1½ | Teaspoon ginger |
| 1 | Teaspoon cinnamon |
| ½ | Cup raisins |

Scald 1 qt. milk in top of double boiler. Combine cornmeal with ½ cup remaining milk and add slowly to scalded milk, stirring constantly. Cook uncovered 20 minutes, stirring constantly. Add molasses, sugar, salt, ginger, cinnamon and raisins. Pour into buttered 1½ qt. baking dish, casserole or beanpot; bake in moderate over (325°) for one hour. Stir in remaining 1½ cups milk and continue baking for 1½ hours.

# Black Bean Soup

| | |
|---|---|
| 1lb. | Package dried black beans, rinsed |
| 6 | Cups of water |
| 1 | Tablespoon olive oil |
| 1 | Cup chopped celery |
| 1 | Large onion, chopped (1 cup) |
| 3 | Garlic cloves, peeled and finely chopped |
| ¾ | Teaspoon dried oregano leaves, crumbled |
| 13¾ oz. | Can chicken broth |
| 3 | ½ inch strips of orange peel (do not include the bitter white part) |
| 1¼ | Teaspoons salt |
| ½ | Teaspoon hot pepper sauce |
| | Sour cream, lemon slices, chopped tomatoes, cooked rice and parsley, for garnish (optional) |

In a large bowl, soak the beans in 5 cups of water overnight. Or, in a large saucepot, bring 5 cups of water and beans to a boil; remove the pan from the heat, cover and let stand for 1 hour.

In a large beanpot, heat the oil in medium heated oven. Stir in the celery, onion, garlic and oregano; cook for 5 to 7 minutes, or until the vegetables are tender.

Add the soaked beans and bean liquid and the remaining 1 cup of water. Bring the mixture to a boil, reduce the heat, cover and simmer for 1 hour, stirring occasionally.

Add the chicken broth, orange peel, salt and hot pepper sauce. Cover and continue cooking 2 to 3 hours longer, or until the beans are tender. Stir every 20 to 30 minutes to prevent the beans from sticking to the bottom of the pan. Add additional water as necessary. Serve the soup in bowls with sour cream, lemon, tomatoes, rice and parsley, if desired.

Makes about 9 cups, 6 to 8 servings.

## Spezzatino Di Agnello Con Patate E Piselli
## Di Numero Uno Chef Compore MarioNocera
## Di Siano, Italy

Lamb Stew with Potatoes and Peas

| | |
|---|---|
| 1-2 lb. | Lamb shank or shoulder chops |
| | Some weight of smooth-skin white potatoes |
| 1 | Onion, sliced thinly |
| 1 | Tablespoon oil (or fat rendered from pancetta {Italian bacon}) |
| ½ | Cup meat stock or tomato sauce or both |
| 1-2 | Cups peas, fresh or fresh-frozen |

**Method:**
On top of stove in a heavy stock pot or fry pan, brown lamb well in oil. Season with salt and pepper. Place browned meat in Boston Beanpot.

In remaining fat, brown lightly potatoes (cut in slices or thick wedges) and onion. Put this mix on top of meat.

Pour stock on top of contents of beanpot. Bake in 300-325° oven for 30 min. Add peas. Mix all well. Recover beanpot and continue baking 15-30 min. more.

Serves 2-4.

Please check with your local store manager ... First Pot Shop products are sold principally throughout specialty and chain stores throughout the U.S.A. which offer the correct and least expensive method of your acquiring them; however, all the reference stores may not carry the full line or stock replacement parts.

For this reason, this mail order section is herein included, but only as a last resort if your local dealer just doesn't have the items.

Credit card customers can order through our internet:
www.potshopofboston.com

All others should send a check, plus the shipping and handling cost as indicated next to the specific item to:

The Pot Shop of Boston
Box 101, Hanover Station
Boston, MA 02113
Phone: 617-523-9210
Fax: 617-523-6765
Web: potshopofboston.com

Please allow up to 30 days from the date of your order for its receipt.

## HOW TO ORDER

IF YOU USE CREDIT CARDS, PLEASE PHONE "THE POT SHOP" AT:
**617-523-9210**
OR FAX US AT:
**617-523-6765**
INDICATING YOUR CREDIT CARD NAME, NUMBER AND ADDRESS <u>EXACTLY</u> AS IT APPEARS ON THE CARD, ALONG WITH THE EXPIRATION DATE AND YOUR DAY TIME AND EVENING PHONE NUMBER, INCLUDING AREA CODE.
INCLUDE A LIST OF ITEMS WANTED AND THE S&H (SHIPPINGAND HANDLING) FOR EACH ITEM.

IF YOU DO NOT USE CREDIT CARDS, PLEASE MAIL CHECKINCLUDING S&H TO:

**THE POT SHOP**
**BOX 101, HANOVER STATION**
**BOSTON, MA 02113**

ALLOW UP TO 30 DAYS FOR RECEIPT OF YOUR ORDER

Ask anyone who's ever done the cooking for a Boston hamand-bean church supper will tell you: You really need a genuine beanpot to make Boston baked beans in the authentic old-fashioned way. For that deliciously slow, sweetly fragrant baking, you want the traditional pot's classic shape and sturdy stoneware protecting your beans from burning or overcooking, while keeping them moist and tasty. Our classic glazed brown-and-white pots and lids are dishwasher-safe. They're versatile for cooking, and even as decorator accents. You get the Official Boston Baked Bean recipe with each pot, and the "Boston Beanpot Cookery" cookbook gives you over 75 other recipes for various meals, including bean-free casseroles and vegetable dishes.

## OUR MOST POPULAR SELLING COMBO

#5233        2 ½ qt. Official Boston Beanpot
each is packed in an attractive gift box with a
recipe

#BK-1        Boston Beanpot Cookery
75 recipes for beans which can be prepared in a
Boston Beanpot other than Boston Baked Beans

#OBBB       A one pound package of the finest beans ever
grown

Entire 3 piece combo $44.85, plus $10.00 for shipping and handling.

# DESIGNED GIFT BOXES

Three sizes come in these very attractive gift boxes with carry case handles: The #5233 – 2 ½ qt., #5258 – 1 ¼ qt., and the #5257 – ¾ qt. The other sizes do not come in these boxes.

Another extremely popular combo is #BK-1, Boston Beanpot Cookery, and #5233, the 2 ½ qt. Beanpot. $41.90, plus s$9.00 shipping and handling.

# THE POT SHOP OFFICIAL BEANPOT LINE

| ITEM | SIZE | PRICE | S&H |
|------|------|-------|-----|
| #5243 | 1 gallon | $49.95 | $12.00 |
| #5239 | 1 pint | $5.95-min. 4pc | $10.00 |
| #5233 | 2 ½ qt. | $29.95 | $10.00 |
| #5258 | 1 ¼ qt. | $19.95 | $ 9.00 |
| #5241 | 5 oz. | $3.96- min 6pc | $10.00 |
| #5257 | ¾ qt. | $14.95 | $ 9.00 |

All beanpots are packed with recipes except the 1 pint and 5oz. Sizes which are used mainly for serving and souvenirs. As a gift, they are truly appreciated.

This super popular cookbook multiplies the number of times your investment in the Official Boston Beanpot brings in a return over 75 delicious, delightful and delectable recipes for your enjoyment.

No. BK-1 - $11.95, Plus $1.75 shipping and handling

# OLD FASHION BROWN AND WHITE EARTHENWARE CUSTARD CUPS

## CUSTARDS – Introduction

"Bring on the dessert. I think I am about to die."
- Last words of Antheime Brillat-Savarin [attrib.]

Ah, what better sweet ending could the encyclopedic chef and food historian A. Brillat-Savarin have had I mind than a light and creamy custard? It is the original comfort food, inherently soothing, unpretentious, perfect in its plainness. A most fitting ending, indeed.

"Baked custard in simple brown custard cups is one of the most familiar, homy (sic) American desserts," we are told in the 1979 revision of the <u>Fannie Farmer Cookbook</u>. No argument there except to point out that many cultures have their variations on what Farmer claims as our own. What is ours alone are the brown-glazed earthenware cups which ideally coddle single custard portions in the water bath used in its preparation.

A custard cup is a 3-inch deep, flat-bottomed, individual-portion cup with slightly flared sides and no handles or covers. They are used to hold custard and pudding while they bake in water. Usually made from porcelain or brown-glazed earthenware, they are distinguished from pot-decrème by the latter's more rounded, lidded, and small handled design.

#5240, set of 6, 8 oz. Each. $23.70, plus $8.00 shipping and handling. Additional pieces $3.95 each. Also great for making popovers.

# OLDE BOSTON CUSTARD CUP COOKERY

**Over 50 delicious, savory, luscious recipes for doing custards in The Pot Shop Stoneware Custard Cups**

## Custard

Take to every pint of Creame; five Egges and put in no whites, and straine your creme and Egges together, season it with Cloves and Mace: and Sugar. And when your paste is well hardened in the Oven, having small Raisins and Dates: put in your stuffe, and let it not bake too much, for muche baking will make your custard to quaile, or els to fall.

-- Source: A.W., A Book of Cookrye - London, 1587

**A Product of The Pot Shop Box 101, Hanover Station Boston, MA 02113 (617) 523-9210 Fax (617) 523-6765**

**$ 11.95**

No. BK-3. Over 50 different delicious, savory custard recipes which can be prepared in The Pot Shop Custard Cups. $11.95, plus $1.75 shipping and handling.

# CASH IN ON CASSEROLES

| 1 quart #5261 | 2 quart #5262 | 3 quart #5263 | 4 quart #5264 | 6 quart #5265 |

The casserole is many things to many people. To some, it's convenience. To the large family, it's the littlest leftover deliciously stretched into an entire meal. To others, it's a lifesaver when busy schedules force dinner into a holding pattern. And still others love casseroles because they hate pots. Added to these reasons for making casseroles goes one other – the dollar. Nowhere else can so much economy be found under one lid – and it's economy of the best sort. The big, hearty servings beautifully disguise the fact that you're watching the budget.

Traditional onion soup shape and color – brown and tan

| Size: | 1 quart | 2 quart | 3 quart | 4 quart | 6 quart |
|-------|---------|---------|---------|---------|---------|
| Item#: | #5261 | #5262 | #5263 | #5264 | #5265 |
| Price: | $14.95 | $24.95 | $34.95 | $49.95 | $69.95 |
| S&H: | $ 7.95 | $ 8.95 | $ 9.95 | $12.95 | $14.95 |

**CASH IN ON CASSEROLES**
**$11.95 - #BK-1**
**$ 1.75 – S&H**
**An absolute must.**
**40 mouthwatering**
**recipes by Merilyn DeVos**

The beauty and symmetry of these casseroles have to be seen to be fully appreciated.

# THE POT SHOP EARTHENWARE PIE PLATE

You'll never use a metal or glass pie plate after using this one – just perfect crust every time.

#5237
Earthenware Pie Plate, $19.95, plus $8.00 S&H

#BK-2
"High on Pie" by Merilyn DeVos, over 75 recipes for baking a multitude of exotic pies, $15.95, plus $2.05 S&H

# THE POT SHOP DOUBLE EGG CUPS

#5244 – Pot Shop Double Egg Cups, one side for those who prefer to eat from the shell, the other larger side for those who don't – brown and tan. $3.95 each, minimum 6 pieces, plus $8.00 S&H

# A POT FULL OF CANDY BEANS
## A GREAT GIFT FOR CANDY LOVERS

Our standard #5233 – 2 ½ qt. Pot filled with candy beans
$49.95, S&H $10.00

Our #5259 – 5 oz. Individual serving beanpot filled with candy bean - $4.50
each – minimum 6 pieces, S&H $10.00.

# THE HISTORY OF OMELETTE PANS

A true omelette pan is made of extremely thick cast aluminum. It is this massive metal which allows the pan to be preheated to a very high temperature before tossing in the butter or other shortening for quick transfer of heat to the egg mixture which then results in the perfect omelette – done in two minutes or less.

In the early 1904's a Midwestern U.S.A. cast aluminum foundry manufactured torpedoes for the U.S. Navy. The front end of the torpedo shell was cut off, so as to allow the explosives, etc., to be inserted. That same front end was approximately 8-11 inches in diameter and shaped like a skillet with shallow sloping sides.

This surplus end piece was simply stock piled in the foundry yard. At some point in the late forties or early 1950's, someone recognized the extraordinary cooking capabilities of the surplus pieces and affixed a handle. They made wonderful omelette pans and were distributed through restaurant supply companies, as there were no gourmet kitchenware stores in existence at that time.

In the 1950's, the Midwestern foundry, for one reason or another, stopped making torpedoes at some point, and the surplus pieces no longer were available.

In 1962, Julia Child, who was just getting started as a television personality, visited The Pot Shop of Boston, one of the finer gourmet kitchenware stores in the U.S.A., explained the above and suggested that Pot Shop management develop a similar heavy cast aluminum omelette pan, since none were then available. Four months later, the first FRENCH CHEF OMELETTE PAN was given to Julia Child at her home in Cambridge, where she used it to do an omelette lunch for Pot Shop management.

As an educator in the field of public broadcasting, she could not officially endorse the omelette pan or any other product.

The Pot Shop has manufactured the FRENCH CHEF OMELETTE PAN ever since that time – now for 40 years.

Now in the opportunistic kitchenware suppliers call anything an omelette pan and present them as such to the extent that it would appear that the market is glutted with omelette pans. Many of these promoters have gone out, more keep coming in who won't be around too long. There is only one FRENCH CHEF OMELETTE PAN. Thousands of people all across the U.S.A. abhor the notion that a true omelette pan exists apart from the FRENCH CHEF OMELETTE PAN made by The Pot Shop, Box 101, Hanover Station, Boston, MA 02113, phone 617-523-9210, fax 617-523-6765, website: www.potshopofboston.com.

Vincent Zarrilli
Founder, The Pot Shop

# JULIA CHILD GOES TORPEDO SHOPPING. (CIRCA 1963)

Julia Child,
Cambridge, MA
Circa 1963

This page is a verbatim reproduction of the "Time Life Cookbook" of the late sixties when Julia Child had the whole country doing Omelettes. At that time, Jacqueline Kennedy gave an omelette party for 500 guests in Washington D.C. It was accommodated by the then Omelette King, Rudolph Stanish of NYC and four other Tuxedo clad omeleteers who performed as each guest stood in one of four lines at a long banquet table. It was a much publicized super soiree.

Shown is the 10" FC10HP
High polish at $99.95
Plus $8.00 S&H.

## To Make Plain or French Omelets

Select one of the tested recipes that follow. Assemble equipment (Fig. 1) and mix ingredients. Heat pan over moderately high heat or as recipe suggests. Pan should
be hot enough to sizzle and foam butter without turning it brown. Use ½ teaspoon butter for cooking a 2 or 3 egg omelet. 1 tablespoon butter for 6 or 8 egg omelet. Rotate pan (Fig. 2) so butter will coat surface evenly. Pour egg mixture (Fig. 3) into pan. Slide pan back and forth slowly over heating unit constantly during cooking. Stir eggs around outside edge of pan with a spatula or a 3 or 4-lined fork (Fig. 4) for about 30 seconds.

Cook eggs until they lose their gloss: let stand 1 or 2 minutes to brown on underside. If a filled omelet is desired, the filling should be added at this time.

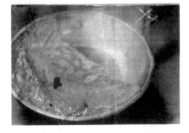

Use the side of the fork to gather
and roll the omelet together.

When the omelet is loosened and
lightly rolled to the side of the
pan,

lift the pan with one hand and
a heated plate with the other.
Gently tilt the pan up and turn the
finished omelet over onto the plate.
Brush the top of the omelet with
butter and serve while it is piping
hot and still just a bit soft inside

## IMPORTANT

Please remember that the French Chef Omelette Pan is made of <u>cast</u> aluminum
which is a relatively porous metal. As such it cannot attain a smooth perfect finish. Consequently, what might appear to be imperfections are not, but are part of
virtually perfect cooking material.

## THE IDEAL CHRISTMAS AND
## FATHER'S DAY GIFT

# THE ORIGINAL FRENCH CHEF OMELETTE PAN

- Born from a suggestion of this eminent Julia Child in 1962.
- Extremely thick cast aluminum.
- Shallow sloping sides.
- Solid wooden handle.
- Instruction booklet with each pan.
- Available in mirror polish finish, black non-stick or natural sand.
- 8 ½" diameter.
- 10 ½" diameter.
- Sells year round for gift giving ... Christmas, Wedding, Birthday, Mother's Day, etc., etc.
- Made entirely in the USA.

ORDERING INFO
HIGH POLISH : FC10-HP-10 ½"
$99.95
HIGH POLISH: FC8-HP – 8 ½"
$59.95
BLACK NON-STICK: BFC10-NS – 10 ½"
$99.95
BLACK NON-STICK: BFC9-NS – 8 ½"
$59.95
NATURAL FINISH: FC8 – 8 ½"
$39.95
NATURAL FINISH: FC10 – 10 ½"
$59 95
(Please add $8.00 PER ITEM for S&H)

A FEW OF THE FAMOUS PEOPLE
WHO HAVE INVESTED IN THE FRENCH
CHEF OMELETTE PAN:

Vincent Price
1966

Joan Fontaine
1964

Jacqueline Kennec
1967

# WHICH ONE TO INVEST IN

The natural finish is rough and porous, definitely non-aesthetic, but its porous nature holds the seasoning very, very well.

## THE WORLD FAMOUS FRENCH CHEF OMELETTE PAN

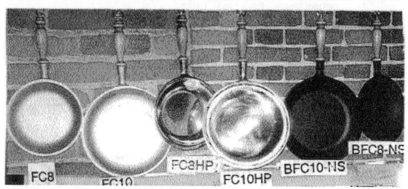

| FC10 | - 8" | Natural Sand Finish | $39.95 |
|------|------|---------------------|--------|
| FC10 | - 10" | Natural Sand Finish | $69.95 |
| FC8HP | - 8" | High Polish | $59.95 |
| FC10HP | - 10" | High Polish | $99.95 |
| BFC10NS | - 10" | Black Non-Stick | $99.95 |
| BFC8NS | - 8" | Black Non-Stick | $59.95 |

All French Chef Omelette Pans are made of the same very thick cast aluminum, but the finish varies. Most people seem to prefer the natural sand finish which is also less expensive, but not for that reason. It is porous and many people feel it holds the seasonings better. The black non-stick seems to be preferred by professional chefs and the high polish are
usually given as gifts.

SINCE ROMAN times, and perhaps earlier, the omelette has been a simple, satisfying meal. In recent American cookbook history, one classic has been written about this ubiquitous dish, and this is it. Like the omelette itself, THE OMELETTE BOOK is useful and always various. Its three hundred recipes will inform a lifetime of omelette making and will entice you to devise your own impromptu variations.

The omelette has been well documented in the literature of food, and Narcissa G. Chamberlain, drawing on her extensive library of old and modern books, condensed and organized this abundance of material from a home cook's point of view. She arranged her chapters under headings resembling a menu; seafood, poultry, meat, vegetables, and (these are a revelation!) desserts; and in each chapter the recipes are usefully alphabetized by major ingredient.

Mrs. Chamberlain discreetly proposed ways to use leftovers, and any sensible reader will pounce on the idea – what a wonderful way to use both eggs and the good things on hand in the refrigerator, whether for an emergency meal or a major production. Precious lobster meat left over? See Omelette Baron de Barante – this is a regal adventure. Choice, small artichokes available at the produce market? Try Artichoke Omelette Provençale a country dish. Something fresh and simple? Watercress Omelette or Omelette Flamande with endive. Something extravagant for New Year's Eve? Look up Caviar. Dessert omelettes begin with Almond and Apricot and end with Melba, Strawberry, and Walnut, with a long and delectable list in between. A picnic? You'll find cold omelettes to go! Also included: the German omelette, the Italian frittata, tiny Russian omelettes, even the almost forgotten Chinese Egg Foo Yung.

If it's an omelette, it's here, along with an entertaining historical introduction in an invaluable culinary companion for your kitchen or by your bedside. NARCISSA G. CHAMBERLAIN collaborated for close to forty years in the publishing ventures of her husband Samuel Chamberlain, printmaker, architectural photographer, writer, and designer of his own books. She produced the recipe manuscripts for three editions for three editions of his gastronomic travel book *Bouquet de France* and of the subsequent *Italian Bouquet* and *British Bouquet*, all published by *Gourmet* magazine. The recipes in *Clémentine* published in 1988. She was a knowledgeable amateur of antiques and pitched in a co-author whenever her husband photographed for books on the interiors of old American homes. Her last book was a comprehensive catalog of her husband's etchings, dry-points, and lithographs, *The Prints of Samuel Chamberlain*, N.A., published by The Boston Public Library in 1984.

#BK—5, $17.95, plus $3.05 S&H
hard cover, over 150 omelette recipes.
Considered the Bible as to omelettes.
The Pot Shop is exclusive U.S.A.
distributor.

Narcissa Chamberlain journeyed from her home in
Marblehead, MA in 1968 to attend a Pot Shop
branch store opening in Boston's Back Bay, where
Omelettes and Martinis were featured. She showed
no interest in the omelettes, but loved the martinis!!!

# THE TEST OF TIME

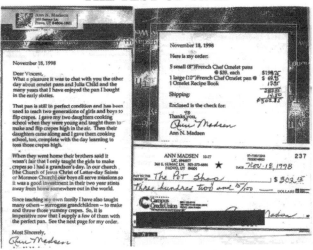

This person purchased the French Chef Omelette Pan in the early sixties when a student at Harvard. Now a grandmother and almost 35 years later, she presented each of her six grandchildren with a Christmas gift of the French Chef Omelette Pan. But she did not break a record. A few years earlier, another grandmother from St. Louis, MO, who had one for 30 years, did the same thing for nine grandchildren. We send a copy of Ann Madsen's order to Julia, who responded. (see below)

**FROM JULIA CHILD'S KITCHEN**

300 Hot Springs Road #1-178, Santa Barbara, CA 93108
Tel: (805) 969 3662
Fax: (805) 969 3946

February 24, 1999

Vincent Zarrilli
The Pot Shop
P.O. Box 101 / Hanover Station
Boston, MA 02113

Dear Vincent:

It was good to hear from you, and I hope we will run into each other one of these days. That was an amusing note from your client, and I am happy to know that she is buying so many omelette pans!

Here's wishing you all the best

*Julia*

# THE POT SHOP SOUFFLE DISH

#5248 – white fluted earthenware 2 quart Soufflé dish – 8" diameter. $19.95, plus $7.50 S&H.

# THE POT SHOP TRADITIONAL ONION
# SOUP BOWLS

#5245 – Extra large, 16 oz. onion soup bowls, with covers. You'll find that onion soup actually tastes better in these bowls which have been in existence for over 100 years and absolutely treasured by their owners. They're great for baking many other things as well. $7.95 each, minimum 4 pieces, plus $8.00 S&H. For more than four pieces, add $1.50 each for S&H.

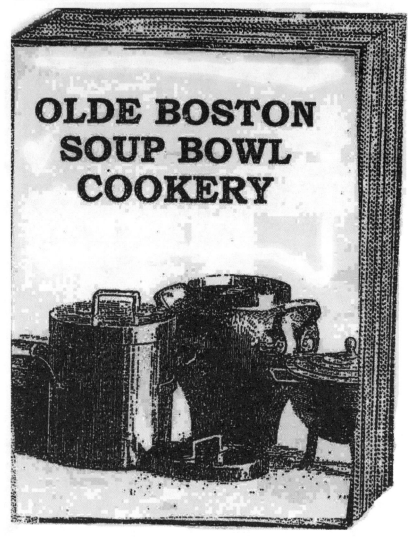

Sixty-three zesty recipes for soups which, to many people, seem to taste even better when served in The Pot Shop Onion Soup Bowls.

#BK-4 - $11.95, plus $1.75 S&H

# NEW ENGLAND TRIGGER MUGS

#5242 - $9.95 each – minimum – 4 pieces. $39.80, plus $8.00 S&H

## The New England Trigger Mug

As legend has it, the colonial sentries drew sustinence from a variety of beverages while on the lookout for the Redcoats in the thick New England woods.

With rifle in one hand and a mug in the other, there was far less spillage when a double handle was added to the mug.

It could be held with a better grip while at the same time allow the sentry to pull the trigger of his musket; hence they were called trigger mugs.

THE POT SHOP
BOX 101, HANOVER STATION
BOSTON, MASSACHUSETTS
02113 U.S.A.
PHONE (617) 523-9210

#5252
Approximately 2 ½" wide by 1" high. The best description is <u>cute</u> and <u>tasteful.</u> A traditional way to serve butter in England with many other uses.
$2.95 ea.,⁻
minimum 8 pieces -
$23.60, plus $7.00
S&H.

# THE POT SHOP PURE CAST IRON
## OVAL SIZZLE PAN

## ABSOLUTELY PERFECT FOR EVERYTHING
## OUTDOORS OR INDOORS

14"x 6 ½" x 1 ¼"

### A Nutritional Benefit: more iron

Cast iron pots and pans have a surprising advantage. Food cooked in unglazed cast iron contains three or more times the iron than food cooked otherwise.

Fajita

**Do bacon 'n eggs. To serve – eat right from pan, which keeps everything hot.**

No. OB-1, $29.95, plus
$8.00 S&H.
A wooden cradle, WC-1
is available for $11.95, plus $2.00 S&H

# THE POT SHOP CHEESE FONDUE POT
#5247 – Brown and white, 2 qt., $24.95, plus $8.00 S&H
## FONDUE NEUCHÂTELOISE

## The Ingredients: (Serves 2)

½ lb.     Switzerland Swiss, shredded, or finely cut
1 ½       tablespoons flour
1         clove fresh garlic
1         cup Neuchâtel win (or any light dry white wine of the Rhine,
Riesling or Chablis types)
          salt, pepper, nutmeg to taste.
1         loaf French or other whit bred with a hard crust (or at lest four
          hard rolls), cut into bite-size pieces each of which must have at
          least one side of crust.
          (Optional) 3 tablespoons Kirschwasser or 2 tablespoons of any
          non-sweetened    fruit brandy such as apple jack, slivowitz,
cognac, etc., or light rum.

## The Preparations:

Dredge cheese with flour. Rub the cooking utensil well with garlic. Pour in the wine and set over very slow fire. When the wine is heated to the point that air bubbles rise to the surface (*never* boiling point), stir with a fork and add the cheese by handfuls, each handful to be completely dissolved before another one is added. Keep stirring until the mixture starts bubbling lightly. At this point add a little salt and pepper and a dash of nutmeg (optional). Finally add and thoroughly stir in the Kirschwasser (or other brandy). Remove the bubbling fondue from the fire and set immediately onto your preheated table heating element.

## The Eating:

Apart from the gustatory enjoyment, there is much inner contentment in a fondue. It requires rather close friendship among the participants because they are literally going to eat out of the same pot! And here's one time when you do your dunking not slyly, but openly and with the full approval of everybody. Spear a piece of bread with a fork, going through the soft part first and securing the points in the crust. Dunk the bread in the fondue in a stirring motion until your neighbor takes over to give you a chance to enjoy your morsel. While each one takes his leisurely turn in rotation, the stirring will help maintain the proper consistency of the fondue and will assure that each piece is thoroughly coated with melted cheese. Care should be taken that the fondue keeps bubbling lightly. This is done by regulating the heat, or by turning it off or on. If the fondue becomes a little too thick at any time, the defect can be rectified by stirring in a little pre-heated (never cold) wine. Towards the end, some of the melted cheese will form a brown crust at the bottom of the utensil. When that happens, keep the heat low in order to prevent the utensil from cracking. The crust can easily be lifted out with a fork and is considered to be a special delicacy. Note: Omit cold or iced drinks during the meal. To those who like it, a pony of Kirschwasser or other brandy may be served. But all should finish with a cup of hot coffee or hot tea.

**No. 6203**
**Stainless steelalcohol stove**
**$19.95, plus$7.95 S&H.**
**This item is perfect for use with**
**The Pot Shop Cheese Fondue**
**(#5247)**

# THE POT SHOP FONDUE BOURGIGNONNE SET

**No. 6202 – All stainless steel Fondue Pot, Alcohol
burner and 6 piece fondue set – all for $49.95, plus $10.00 S&H.**

**<u>FONDUE PLATES</u>
No. 6201 – 6 piece fondue dish set. Smooth
high gloss black color, 4 sauce sections,
$48.00, plus $12.00 S&H**
*Raw beef cube section ,Remaining sections are for
sauces, condiments, etc
Made of pure stoneware and very durable.  Available in
off white.*

## The Fondue Rule Book makes a well-appreciated gift for your special friend

BK-6 – The Fondue Rule Book, $15.95, plus $1.75 S&H
If you wish to buy more than one, please take 20% off for each
additional book – no limit.

# MAIL ORDER FORM
# TEAR OUT AND SEND IN

**THE POT SHOP, PO BOX 101
HANOVER STATION, BOSTON, MA 02113
PHONE 617-523-9210
FAX 617-523-6765
WEBSITE: WWW.POTSHOPOFBOSTON.COM**

Date:_____

Purchaser
Name:_____

Address:_____

_____Zip_____

To be sent to:

Name:_____

Address:_____

_____Zip_____

| QTY. | ITEM | STOCK NO. | PRICE EACH | S&H | TOTAL PRICE |
|------|------|-----------|------------|-----|-------------|
|      |      |           |            |     |             |
|      |      |           |            |     |             |
|      |      |           |            |     |             |
|      |      |  TOTALS   |            |     |             |

Postage & Handling                    _____

Shipping and Handling, only MA residents       _____
Pay 5% sales tax
No sales tax unless you are a MA resident
TOTAL ENCLOSED _____